a poem is a mirror walking down a strange street

e e *cummings*

Acknowledgements

The authors wish to thank the many teachers and students who have worked with them to develop these materials.

The authors and publishers are grateful for permission to use the following copyright material:

Fleur Adcock: 'For A Five-Year-Old'. Reprinted from Fleur Adcock's *Selected Poems* (1983) by permission of Oxford University Press. 'The Telephone Call'. © Fleur Adcock 1986. Reprinted from *The Incident Book* by Fleur Adcock (1986) by permission of Oxford University Press.

Maya Angelou: 'On Aging', from *And Still I Rise* © 1987 by Maya Angelou and 'The Health-Food Diner' from *Shaker, why don't you sing* © 1983 by Maya Angelou. Reprinted by permission of Virago Press. For the recording: 'On Aging' from *And Still I Rise* by Maya Angelou. Copyright © 1978 by Maya Angelou. Reprinted by permission of Random House, Inc. 'The Health Food Diner' from *Shaker, why don't you sing* by Maya Angelou. Copyright © 1983 by Maya Angelou. Reprinted by permission of Random House, Inc.

Carol Ann Duffy: 'Who Loves Who' from *The Other Country* (1990) and 'Talent' from *Standing Female Nude* (1985). Reprinted by permission of Anvil Press Poetry.

Robert Frost: 'Fire and Ice' from *The Poetry of Robert Frost* edited by Edward Connery Lathem. Reprinted on behalf of the Estate of Robert Frost by Jonathan Cape.

Carole E. Gregory: 'Love Letter'. Reprinted by permission of Virago Press.

Adrian Henri: 'Salad Poem' from *Collected Poems* (1986). Reprinted by permission of Allison & Busby.

Langston Hughes: 'Ku Klux'. Copyright 1942 by Alfred A. Knopf, Inc. Reprinted from *Selected Poems Of Langston Hughes*, by permission of the publisher.

Elizabeth Jennings: 'Performer' from *Collected Poems*. Reprinted by permission of Carcanet.

Meiling Jin: 'World Geography and the Rainbow Alliance' from *Black Women Talk Poetry* (1987) published by Blackwoman Talk. Reprinted by permission of the author.

Denise Levertov: 'Living' from *O Taste And See* (1963). Reprinted by permission of New Directions Publishing Corporation.

Roger McGough: 'Poem about the sun slinking off and putting up a notice' from *Watchwords*, and 'Happiness' from *Gig*. Reprinted by permission of Jonathan Cape Publishers.

Judith Nichols: 'Classifying' from *Midnight Forests And Other Poems*, Reprinted by permission of Faber & Faber Ltd.

Theodore Roethke: 'Ballad of the Clairvoyant Widow' from *The Collected Poems of Theodore Roethke*. Reprinted by permission of Faber & Faber Ltd.

Ulrich Schaffer: 'Let's Talk About It' from *For the Love of Children*. Reprinted by permission of Lion Publishing.

Stevie Smith: 'Not Waving But Drowning' from *The Collected Poems Of Stevie Smith* published by Penguin 20th Century Classics. Reprinted by permission of James MacGibbon, Literary Executor.

The publishers wish to thank the following for permission to reproduce photographs:

Aldus Archive/Syndication International
Barnabys Picture Library
John Birdsall
Bridgeman Art Library/*Tropical Storm with Tiger* reproduced by courtesy of The Trustees, The National Gallery, London
Colorsport
Sally and Richard Greenhill
Image Bank/Larry Dale Gordon
Impact/Ben Edwards, Robin Lubbock, Homer Sykes
Oxford Scientific
Photo Co-op/Crispin Hughes, Rob Scott

The publishers have made every effort to contact the copyright holder of the Ku Klux Klan photograph, but have been unable to do so. If the copyright holder would like to contact the publishers, the publishers would be happy to pay an appropriate reproduction fee.

Location photography by Rob Judges

Illustrations by:

Nancy Anderson
Caroline Church
Clare Jarrett
Felicity Roma Bowers
Susan Scott

The picture on the cover is *Bridge at Sèvres* by Henri Rousseau, reproduced by permission of The Courtauld Institute of Art.

Contents

To Students

The poems in this anthology have been chosen to give you a taste of the interesting variety of contemporary poetry written in English. Through the poems and the activities in the book, we hope that you will not only improve your English, but discover that poetry is easy and enjoyable to listen to or read.

Poetry can extend your understanding of yourself and of the world in which you live. People who do not normally read poetry are often surprised to find that it has a great deal to do with their ordinary lives, and does not belong only on dusty shelves in university libraries.

Don't be too worried if you don't understand everything immediately; even native speakers read and re-read poems, discovering new levels of meaning as they do so. Listening to the cassette can also help bring out new levels of meaning, as well as increase your familiarity with the oral dimension of poetry and language.

You will be asked to do many speaking and writing activities in pairs and small groups. In this way you can benefit from the knowledge and experience of others in your class. But don't forget that they want to hear from you as well. Talking about poetry is an area where there is no right answer, so expressing your opinion, even if it is not in perfect English, can help other people understand the poems.

Above all, we hope that the book will make you want to continue to read poetry. Don't be too discouraged if it seems a bit difficult at first. Many people feel some irritation when the meaning of a poem seems to escape them, but in the end they find that reading it has been a rewarding and worthwhile experience. Even poets feel this. As Marianne Moore says in her poem:

Poetry

I, too, dislike it.
Reading it, however, with a perfect contempt for it, one discovers in it, after all, a place for the genuine.

Joanne Collie

Gillian Porter Ladousse

To Teachers

What is this book?

An anthology of poetry and a resource book of ideas for using poetry in the classroom. Its aim is twofold: to help learners read and enjoy poems as works of art, and to help them develop their fluency skills in the new language. It is accompanied by a cassette to help comprehension and to provide a link between spoken and written forms of poetry.

What level is the book for?

The book can be used with students from an intermediate level upwards. The activities that we propose usually include at least one which is designed to help students understand the gist of the poem and respond to it. At this level, it may be that some of the poem's subtleties are not fully perceived, especially in the first few readings. However, even native speakers re-read poems and find new levels of meaning on each successive occasion. We would like to encourage students to see their reading of poetry in this same light.

The assumption behind the writing and discussion activities is that affective response has an important place in learning languages. Communicating messages or expressing their own reaction, even imperfectly, is a vital part of students' development at any level.

Why use poetry at this level?

Why not use it? People enjoy poetry and have always done so. With its strong oral element, its musical quality, its emotional and imaginative impact, it is a basic form of human communication.

Teachers sometimes feel that poetry is too difficult, or not as useful as everyday language. However, many people are increasingly finding that the functional language that is the basis of many syllabuses is impersonal. It lacks the affective dimension that enables learners to build up their own association with the new language and their ability to use it fluently. Furthermore, what is sometimes considered as 'deviant' language in poetry can free learners from the inhibiting assumption that there is only one, right way of saying things. We emphasize the way that poems relate to people's lives, allowing learners to give their own personal response within a non-threatening framework.

Poetry will obviously not replace mainstream vocabulary and structure work in any classroom, but has an important role to play alongside it.

Why these particular poems?

This anthology is a personal choice of poems we like and have used successfully with language learners and with teachers. They address the concerns of many people and combine intrinsic interest with good possibilities for exploitation in the classroom. We hope that the selection will facilitate the often arduous task of finding appropriate poems and adapting them for particular classes.

How are the poems presented?

Each poem is presented with activities which can usually be fitted into a one-hour teaching period and with follow-up activities which can be done in a later period or for homework. The poems are presented within the following general framework of activities.

Focussing: most poems are preceded by warm-up activities to be done before the poem is read or listened to. These enable learners to associate the theme of the poem with their own lives.

Listening to and reading the poem: the next set of activities helps students to understand the overall meaning and respond to what is special in the poem. Response activities are usually woven into comprehension work; the student needs to be able to understand the language in order to respond. But a further aim is to encourage students to be aware of the literary qualities which characterize that particular work of art. Students should be encouraged to listen to and read the poem several times before beginning the activities which follow. Recordings on the tape are shown by the symbol T.

Follow-up: the final activities usually ask students to produce a short piece of writing based on their own response or on the group work they have done. We have given suggestions for each poem, but we hope that teachers will use their own ideas for further work, if appropriate. For example, students can be asked to find visual material to illustrate the poems. They could keep diaries or on-going logs to record their reactions to the poems.

In some cases the final exercise asks students to write a poem. If they think of poetry as necessarily bound by rigid rules of rhythm or rhyme, they may find this daunting. They should be encouraged to concentrate on expressing their emotions, rather than trying to fit their words into set patterns. A simple format, however, can sometimes be helpful. Students often enjoy writing Haiku (a poem of 17 syllables in lines of 5, 7 and 5 syllables derived from a Japanese form) or other poems with specific numbers of syllables. Using very short lines beginning with the letters of a title is another way of stimulating the imagination. The example on the left, for *Fire and Ice*, was written by a student in one of our poetry workshops.

Ice and Fire

Isolation
Coldness
Emptiness, feelings that I
Feel
In this
Reckless
Endless night . . .

What should be done about difficult vocabulary?

Most of the poems in this anthology contain some words that students will not have come across before. In the initial phase, it is important for them to focus on what they do understand rather than what they don't. Students can also be encouraged to use the context to pick up meanings. For these reasons, we think it is better not to isolate possibly difficult vocabulary before reading and listening to the poem. Very often, the warm-up activities will introduce not only the words but also the concepts that students need to understand and enjoy the poem. The comprehension activities then give further practice with the new vocabulary.

Some teachers prefer to pre-teach vocabulary items which they think will prove particularly difficult for their own students. Words which might need to be pre-taught are listed in the teacher's notes at the back. Class teachers are usually in a better position to appreciate their own learners' difficulties and assess the kind of help necessary for each poem.

In a few cases, the poems have unusual or culture-specific words which would not be particularly useful for students to learn as part of their active vocabulary. These words are not stressed in the activities, but simply glossed for the teacher at the back. When the information is passed on to students, it may be useful to remind them that not every word they meet has to be learnt and remembered.

Why is the learner's response so important?

Learners are encouraged to have their own ideas and not rely on the teacher's 'authoritative' interpretation. This is not meant to discourage teachers from giving their own opinion or providing information which may help learners shape their own views. However, we do resist the idea of a single, canonical, right view. We ourselves have not always agreed about what poems say, but the resulting discussions have always been fruitful and made us return to the poems with a new perspective. Our practice in this is consistent with modern critical theory which has insisted on the intertextual re-creation that occurs with every new reading of a literary text.

How important is group work?

Most of the activities in this book suggest pair work or group work. Learners can often discover and extend their individual response by discussing the poem with others. In addition, the views of other students can significantly enrich and diversify their own. However, poetry touches upon some of our most personal feelings. It is important to incorporate into the lesson some periods when the poem can be re-read or listened to quietly.

We hope you will enjoy using these poems, adapting the activities to suit your own teaching situation. We also hope that working with this anthology will give you ideas for exploiting other poems that you like. Finally, we hope that working through our activities will make your students more confident in their own ability to read and enjoy poetry.

happiness

I What is happiness?

What is your idea of happiness?

Work with a partner. Do any of the pictures represent happiness for you? Why? On the list below, tick [√] the things which make you feel happy. Add anything else which seems very important to you. Show your list to a partner. What is the same on your lists and what is different? Can you agree on the two most important items?

winning a lot of money
someone to love
a hug from a child
being on top of a mountain
birds singing in the morning
a large, fast car
staying in bed on Sunday

getting a fabulous job
listening to your favourite
 music
a child's first words
a palm-fringed beach
the house of your dreams
a hot day in summer

a meal in your favourite
 restaurant
a smile from an unknown
 person
someone says something nice
 to you
passing a difficult exam

_____

_____

_____

_____

_____

_____

happiness

lying in bed ofa weekday morning
Autumn
and the trees
none the worse for it.
Youve just got up   5
to make tea toast and a bottle
leaving pastures warm
for me to stretch into

in his cot
the littlefella   10
outsings the birds

Plenty of honey in the cupboard.
Nice.

Roger McGough

II A particular view of happiness

T Listen to the poem while you read it.

Listen again, and cross out the information which you feel is
not true in the following sentences:

1 The person who is speaking in
  the poem is alone / not alone.
2 The leaves on the trees have
  begun to fall / haven't begun
  to fall yet.
3 The bottle is for the baby / for
  the person in bed.

4 One person stays in bed
  comfortably / both people get up.
5 The baby is asleep / awake.
6 There is a lot of honey in the
  cupboard / the home offers
  everything needed to make the
  speaker happy.

Compare your answers with your partner's. Now rewrite the
poem in complete sentences with normal spaces between words
and standard punctuation.

When you have finished, join up with another pair. Are the
paragraphs that you have written the same? Compare the poem
and your paragraphs. What are the differences between them?
What are the effects of the way the poet has set out his poem?

III My view of happiness is . . .

Think about a moment in your life when you were happy.
Imagine that you are back in that situation. Here are some
questions to help you recreate the moment:

Where are you?   What are you doing?
What time of day is it?   What are other people doing?
What time of the year is it?   What feelings do you have . . . ?
Are you with anyone?

Now write a few sentences about that moment.

Sit with a partner. Read your sentences to each other. Pin up
your sentences or read them to other people in your class.

Salad Poem

1 Painting a picture

Think about an object or a person that makes you happy.
Imagine you are painting a picture of what is in your mind.
Look at the blank canvas above.

Where is the object or person on your canvas?
What are the main colours?
Is there anything else on the canvas?

Work in pairs. Find out what is on your partner's canvas by
asking questions.

Is there an object on the canvas?
Is there a person or animal?
Is there a landscape?
Is there anything in the very centre of the canvas?
Is there anything happening?
What is the main colour?
Is everything on the canvas close, or are some things far away?

Now describe your own canvas by answering your partner's
questions.

Salad Poem

(for Henri Rousseau le Douanier)

The sun is shining outside
Henri Rousseau (Gentil Rousseau)
The sky is blue
   like your skies
I want to paint the salad   5
on the table
bright crisp green red purple
lettuce and radishes, ham and tomatoes
Paint them like your jungles
Gentle Rousseau   10
I want to paint
   All things bright and beautiful
   All salads great and small
I want to make
   Blue skies bluer   15
   Green grass greener
   Pink flowers brighter
      Like you
         Henri Rousseau

Adrian Henri

The National Gallery, London

II Are poems like paintings?

T Listen to the poem while you read it.

Work with a partner to fill in the questionnaire on the next page. You may not know all the answers, but have a guess and see if other people in the class can help you.

Questionnaire
Tick the right answers.

1 Henri Rousseau was a nineteenth-century painter who was also
__ *a customs officer.*
__ *a philosopher.*
__ *a zookeeper.*

2 Henri Rousseau painted
__ *abstract pictures.*
__ *naïve paintings with brilliant colours.*
__ *light-coloured scenery with water.*

3 Jean-Jacques Rousseau was
__ *a French chef.*
__ *a seventeenth-century painter of nature.*
__ *an eighteenth-century philosopher.*

4 In England, a salad is usually
__ *lettuce.*
__ *vegetables chopped up with a dressing.*
__ *a plate of cold food.*

*5 **All things bright and beautiful** is a quotation from*
__ *the Bible.*
__ *a child's nursery rhyme.*
__ *an English hymn.*

*6 The original line for **All salads great and small** is*
__ ***All people great and small.***
__ ***All creatures great and small.***
__ ***All species great and small.***

7 Adrian Henri is
__ *a Liverpool poet.*
__ *a freelance painter.*
__ *a singer/songwriter.*

III Gentle Rousseau

The speaker of the poem likes Henri Rousseau for many different reasons.
In small groups, decide which of these reasons you feel is the most important. Can you add any other reasons?

Adrian Henri shares a name with Henri Rousseau.
The paintings are full of bright colours.
The paintings are more vibrant and intense than real life.
The painter creates his own world.
Any other reason: _____

What about you? Do you like the paintings of Henri Rousseau? Are there any other painters in your own country you like for the same reasons? Compare your ideas with others.

IV Dear . . .

Think of someone you admire: someone who has had an influence on your own life, or someone who has changed the world. Write a letter to that person, saying what you admire and what you hope to do in your own life.

Classifying

I What have we got in common?

In pairs, think of ways of classifying the people in your class.
For example:

male / female
people who wear glasses / people who don't wear glasses
dark hair / light hair
like sport / don't like sport
shy / outgoing

Now add more categories of your own.

In groups of four or five, compare your lists of categories.
Choose five of them and write them below:

1 _____ *2* _____ *3* _____ *4* _____ *5* _____

How do the people in your group fit into these categories? Write
their names under any of the five headings which apply to them.

Classifying

Philip and Annie wear glasses
and so do Jim and Sue,
but Jim and Sue have freckles,
and Tracey and Sammy too.
Philip and Jim are in boys' group   5
but Philip is tall like Sam
whilst Jim is small like Tracey and Sue
and Clare and Bill and Fran.
Sue is in Guides and Recorders,
but Clare is in Guides and football   10
whilst Helen fits in most things –
except she's a girl and quite tall.
Jenny is curly and blonde and short
whilst Sally is curly but dark;
Jenny likes netball, writing and maths   15
but Sally likes no kind of work.
Philip and Sam are both jolly,
Fran's best for a quiet chat;
now I
   have freckles, like joking, am tall, curly, dark, in Guides, football   20
and play penny whistles and the piano . . .

how do *I* fit into all that?

Judith Nichols

II Classifying

T   Listen to the poem while you read it.
The author has made a diagram to show what the people in the poem have in common. With a partner, can you add the names that are missing? They are written underneath.

Some of the categories have been left out. Which ones are they? Why has the author left them out?

Annie

Tracey

Jenny

Helen

Clare

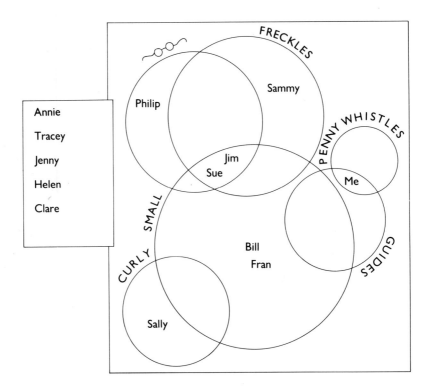

III Overlapping categories

In your groups of four or five, can you make a diagram like the one above to show some of the things you have in common?

What are the ways in which we categorize people in our daily lives? For example, what are the most common stereotypes on television, in newspapers, in advertisements, and so on? Which of the categories are positive? Which are negative? Make two lists and compare them with those of other groups.

IV Individuals are special

On a card, write something about yourself that you think is completely different from everybody else in your class and one thing that you think you share with only a few people. Do not write your name on it. Give it to your teacher, who will mix them up and give you another card back. Interview the people in your class to find out whose card you have got.

Let's Talk About It

I know
that you think
you know
what is good for me,
but   5
I also think
that I know
what is good for me.

I know
you mean well,   10
but
I also mean well
for myself,
and in the end
I have to live my life.   15

. . .

Ulrich Schaffer

I Shall we talk about it?

☐ Listen to the poem while you read it.

In pairs, talk about these questions:

In the poem, who could the I and the you be?
What is their relationship? Are they friendly, loving, caring,
resentful or hostile towards each other?

Ask your teacher or other students if you need other words to
describe the relationship.

II How does it end?

The last stanza of the poem is missing. How do you think it
continues? Do other pairs or groups agree?

☐ When you have compared your ideas, listen to the last
stanza. Is it similar to what you imagined, or different?

III Replying

With a partner, think about situations where you give advice. Note down the kind of remarks you use when you are giving advice and think you know best. See what other groups have written. Are your remarks more dramatic or forceful than the language in the poem?

Now imagine you are the person spoken to in the poem. Write a reply. Try to keep the language as ordinary and neutral as in the poem.

IV Finding something better

With another student, look at these situations. Choose one, adopt the roles, and together prepare a conversation between the two characters.

Situation 1
Role A You are a young person who likes staying out late at discos and parties.
Role B You are a parent whose child stays out late at night. You feel that this is dangerous and bad for school work.

Situation 2
Role A You are married and have looked after the children for the last ten years. Now they are grown up, you want to go back to work.
Role B Your spouse wants to go back to work after ten years of looking after the children. You feel that going back to work will be too stressful and is in any case unnecessary.

Situation 3
Role A You are thinking of getting divorced and are talking about it with a friend.
Role B Your friend is thinking of getting divorced but you feel very strongly that it would be a mistake.

Situation 4
Role A You have been offered a very good job on a different continent and are keen to go. You are talking to a parent about it.
Role B Your daughter or son wants to emigrate to a new continent and you are sure that this is the wrong thing to do.

Situation 5
Role A You have been living in the country but are attracted by better career prospects in a city. The person you live with is not keen to move.
Role B You enjoy living in the country but the person you are living with is very eager to move to a city. You feel such a move would be a disaster.

When you are ready, join up with another group and in turn act out your conversation. The other group will listen to both sides of the story. What do they think the people in your story ought to do next? Can they offer advice? What do you think of this advice?

On Aging

I How old is old?

Which of these people are young? Which are middle-aged?
Which are old? Compare your views with a partner's. How do
you decide?

Work through this questionnaire with a partner. Imagine each
situation and talk about it. How do your reactions differ? Do
the two of you agree with other people in your class?

Questionnaire: what do you feel about old age?
Tick [√] your own opinion.

1 *Anna is an only child and is single. She has an interesting
and busy professional life. Her mother is eighty years old
and a widow. The mother should:*
__ *live with Anna.*
__ *go to an old people's home.*
__ *have a 'granny flat' (an independent flat) in Anna's house.*
__ *find another solution:* _____

2 *When you have a problem in your life, who do you talk it
over with?*
__ *a good friend*
__ *a parent*
__ *your grandparent or an older relation*
__ *someone else:* _____

3 *What present would you give an elderly woman for her
birthday?*
__ *a rocking chair*
__ *a bar of scented soap*
__ *a bed jacket*
__ *a camera*
__ *something else:* _____

continued 15

4 What present would you give an elderly man for his birthday?
___ *a video*
___ *a pipe*
___ *a walking stick*
___ *a bicycle*
___ *something else:* _____

5 Two elderly people are waiting to cross the road. What do you do?
___ *Offer to help them.*
___ *Think they need no help.*
___ *Hurry past them.*
___ *Do something else:* _____

6 A good holiday for an elderly couple is:
___ *two weeks in a cottage by the sea.*
___ *a walking tour in the mountains.*
___ *a package coach trip.*
___ *something else:* _____

On Aging

When you see me sitting quietly,
Like a sack on the shelf,
Don't think I need your chattering.
I'm listening to myself.
Hold! Stop! Don't pity me!   5
Hold! Stop your sympathy!
Understanding if you've got it,
Otherwise I'll do without it!

When my bones are stiff and aching
And my feet won't climb the stair,   10
I will only ask one favor:
Don't bring me no rocking chair.

When you see me walking, stumbling,
Don't study and get it wrong.
'Cause tired don't mean lazy   15
And every goodbye ain't gone.
I'm the same person I was back then,
A little less hair, a little less chin,
A lot less lungs and much less wind.
But ain't I lucky I can still breathe in.   20

Maya Angelou

II On Aging

T Read the poem, while you listen to it. It is read first by a woman, then by a man.

Work with a partner. Look at these two sentence beginnings:

1	*2*
The speaker in the poem thinks:	The speaker imagines other people thinking:
I am a person who . . . **wants to be independent.**	*The speaker is a person who . . .* **likes to hear people talking.**

Now look at this list. Which endings go with which of the beginnings? Put each ending in column 1 or column 2. Some may go in both. An example has been done for you.

likes to hear people talking.
likes to spend a quiet time thinking.
seems quiet and must be sad.
is slow and not too energetic.
is tired but hasn't given up.
doesn't want to do anything any more.
is lonely.
wants to be independent.
hasn't changed inside.
is full of aches and pains.
is very determined.
is happy to be alive.
is nearing death.

Compare with other groups. If you have made different choices, explain why.

III Imagining the speaker

Which of the two recordings of the poem did you prefer? Compare your choice with other students. What in the poem makes you think the speaker is really a man or a woman?

Which of the following expressions tells you that this is a black American talking?

Don't bring me no rocking chair
'Cause tired don't mean lazy
Don't think I need your chattering

And every goodbye ain't gone
Otherwise I'll do without it

IV A centenary

You are a reporter and are going to interview somebody who is 100 years old today. Work with a partner to decide what questions you will ask. Write your questions.

Change partners. Take these roles in turn:
Role A: You are a reporter interviewing someone who is 100 years old today.
Role B: You are 100 years old today. A reporter from the local newspaper comes to interview you.

V The interview

Either write the interview together, as a short article for a local newspaper, or record it on a tape. Read it or play it to another group.

poem about the sun slinking off and pinning up a notice

I A change of view

Look out of the window of your classroom. What can you see? Imagine how that scene could change. The change could be the result of:

1 an expected event, like the coming of winter or summer
2 an unexpected but possible event, like an earthquake
3 a totally fantastic event, like an invasion from outer space.

With a partner, choose one of the three types of events. Prepare a description of what the scene would look like after the event you imagine.

Compare with other groups.

poem about the sun slinking off and pinning up a notice

the sun
hasn't got me fooled
not for a minute
just when
you're beginning to believe   5
that   grass is green
and   skies are blue
and   colour is king
hey   ding a ding ding
and   10
        a
           host
              of
                 other
                    golden
                       etceteras   15
before you know where you are
he's slunk off somewhere
and pinned up a notice saying

MOON

Roger McGough

II Slinking off

T Listen to the poem while you read it.

With a partner, match each one of the expressions in the
column on the left with its meaning in the column on the right.
Use the poem to help you.

1 to slink off	*a* to make someone believe something that is not true
2 to pin up a notice	*b* suddenly
3 to have somebody fooled	*c* place information in public view
4 colour is king	*d* a part of a song that is repeated
5 hey ding a ding ding	*e* things in bright sunshine
6 a host	*f* to go away secretly
7 golden etceteras	*g* many
8 before you know where you are	*h* everything brightly coloured

Check your answers with another group.

III Nature's notices

Work in a small group. Match these situations with the right
notice:

a yellowing leaves on the trees   *d* yellowing grass
b an empty flower bed   *e* daffodils blooming
c dark clouds in the sky

Can you fill in the three empty signs for other situations in
nature? Show your signs to another group and ask them to
guess your situations.

IV Shape poems

What is your reaction to the shape of the poem? Do you like it?
Does it have a meaning? Exchange ideas with others in the
class.

With a partner, write your own short poem about nature in an
appropriate shape.

For a Five-year-old

1 **Creepy crawlies**

If you find any of these in your bedroom, which do you kill and which do you protect?

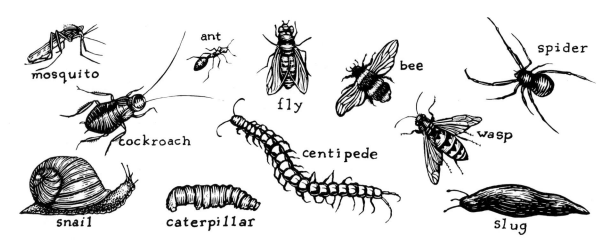

In small groups, talk about your reaction to these creatures. Can you all agree?

For a Five-year-old

A snail is climbing up the window-sill
Into your room, after a night of rain.
You call me in to see, and I explain
That it would be unkind to leave it there:
It might crawl to the floor; we must take care   5
That no one squashes it. You understand,
And carry it outside, with careful hand,
To eat a daffodil.

I see, then, that a kind of faith prevails:
Your gentleness is moulded still by words   10
From me, who have trapped mice and shot wild birds,
From me, who drowned your kittens, who betrayed
Your closest relatives, and who purveyed
The harshest kind of truth to many another.
But that is how things are: I am your mother   15
And we are kind to snails.

Fleur Adcock

II What we say

T Listen to the first stanza of the poem. What is the mother saying or implying about life? With a partner, choose the sentences that seem appropriate.

It's important to protect life, however small.
Animals in bedrooms are dangerous for your health.
Children should imitate their parents.
You should be kind to animals.
It's disgusting to have small animals crawling on the floor.
Children must learn from the example of parents.
Children must learn from what parents tell them.
We should be careful not to destroy the natural world, even by accident.

Compare with another pair. What do you feel about the mother's attitude?

III What we do

T Listen to the whole poem while you read it. Draw a line to connect each one of the expressions on the left with its meaning on the right.

a kind of faith prevails	I have done wrong to members of our family.
your gentleness is moulded still by words from me	I told people things that were true but unpleasant.
me who drowned your kittens	You believe what I say.
me who betrayed your closest relatives	I killed your pets.
me who purveyed the harshest kind of truth to many another	You are kind because I tell you to be kind.

Check your answers with a partner.

In the second stanza, the mother admits that she has done five cruel things. With your partner, decide which of these is the most cruel and which is the least cruel.
Have most people in the class made the same choices as you?

IV Do as I say and not as I do

T Listen to people talking about the contradiction between what their parents said and what their parents did.
In small groups, talk about the situations. Did anything similar happen in your family?

Choose one of the situations you heard, or one of your own. With a partner, write a short dialogue of the situation. Get together with another pair and act out your dialogues to each other.

Fire and Ice

I Stories of fire or ice

Work in small groups. Think about fire or ice. Can you remember any striking stories involving either fire or ice – from real life, mythology, fairy tales, history, novels or films? Tell each other your stories. Then consult with the class. Did anyone hear a story that the whole class should listen to? Ask that person to tell it.

As a class, what positive and negative aspects of fire or ice did your stories show? List them under these headings:

+ Fire	– Fire		+ Ice	– Ice

Fire and Ice

Some say the world will end in fire,
Some say in ice.
From what I've tasted of desire
I hold with those who favor fire.
But if it had to perish twice,   5
I think I know enough of hate
To say that for destruction ice
Is also great
And would suffice.

Robert Frost

II Fire and Ice

T Listen to the poem while you read it.

With a partner, find the words, expressions or lines in the poem
that contain a meaning close to each of these statements.

1 Passion can be as strong as fire.
2 Hatred is a cold emotion.
3 Some people think that a new ice age will put an end to life
   on earth.
4 Hatred is destructive, but not as destructive as passion.
5 Desire is totally destructive.
6 The speaker has seen hatred at work.
7 Some scientists believe that the sun will eventually burn up
   the world.
8 The speaker has had some experience of passion.

Check your answers with other groups. Have you all got the
same answers? Which do you think is worse: fire or ice? passion
or hatred? Do you all agree?

III A trial of fire and ice

Work in pairs. Imagine that there is to be a trial of fire and ice,
to decide whether or not to ban them from the earth. Choose
one of the following roles:

Role A: You are the two lawyers against fire. Write a few
sentences attacking it.
Role B: You are the two lawyers for fire. Write a few sentences
defending it.
Role C: You are the two lawyers against ice. Write a few
sentences attacking it.
Role D: You are the two lawyers for ice. Write a few sentences
defending it.

Present your opposing cases to the class. When all the students
have presented their cases, the class votes for either banning or
keeping fire and ice.

23

Love Letter

1 The story of Samson and Delilah

Look at the list below. If there are any words you don't know, check with other students.

extraordinary strength
thousands killed
city gates
eleven hundred pieces of silver
hair cut off
a prison
a feast
a temple
pillars

T Listen to the story of Samson and Delilah. Make notes as you listen. With a partner, retell the story, making sure you include all the words above.

24

Love Letter

Dear Samson,
I put your hair
in a jar
by the pear tree
near the well.   5
I been thinkin'
over what I done
and I still don't think
God gave you
all that strength   10
for you to kill
my people.

Love — Delilah

Carole E Gregory

II A love letter?

T Listen to the poem while you read it. Whose point of view is it?

With another student, talk about the following questions:
1 Why does Delilah act in the way she does: in the Bible? in the poem? Are the reasons the same?
2 Is the poem really a 'love letter'?
3 What are Delilah's emotions? Is she caring, loving, resentful, remorseful, triumphant, sorrowful . . . ?
Exchange ideas with other groups.

III Who's the culprit?

Work in a small group. Look at these parts of the story. What do you think about each one of these actions? Do you think they were good things to do – or bad things to do? In front of each one, put a number from 1 to 5: 1 = very bad; 2 = bad; 3 = understandable; 4 = acceptable; 5 = admirable. For example, if you think that it is understandable that Delilah takes money from the Philistines, put 3 for that action.

__ Samson kills thousands of Philistines.
__ The Philistines promise money to Delilah.
__ Delilah takes money from the Philistines.
__ Samson lies three times to Delilah about his secret.
__ Samson tells Delilah his secret when she asks him again and again.
__ People laugh at blind Samson.
__ Samson kills himself and thousands of Philistines.

IV The other side of the story

Think of a story which is usually told from the point of view of a hero or heroine struggling against a villain. In your group, imagine how the villain feels. Discuss how the story could be told from the villain's point of view. Tell the class your story.

The Grey Squirrel

I Appearances can be deceptive

Things are sometimes beautiful but deadly. With a partner, match each picture with the danger(s) that may be hidden within it.

It can make breathing difficult.
It can contain very hot liquid.
It can maul people to death.
It can electrocute you.
It can let you fall to your death.
It can contain a bomb.
It can make you die of cold.
It can poke your eye out.
It can make you drown.
It can be poisonous.
It can cause severe injury.

With your partner, make a list of some other beautiful things which can hide danger. Give your list to another group. Ask them to talk about all the possible dangers hidden in your list.

The Grey Squirrel

Like a small grey
coffee-pot
sits the squirrel.
He is not

all he should be,   5
kills by dozens
trees, and eats
his red-brown cousins.

The keeper on the
other hand,   10
who shot him, is
a Christian, and

loves his enemies,
which shows
the squirrel was not   15
one of those.

Humbert Wolfe

II The Grey Squirrel

T Listen to the poem while you read it.

The poem is very ironical – what it says literally is often different from what it suggests. Work in pairs. For each of the following statements, put S if it is a similar meaning to the poem, or D if its meaning is different.

1 __ The squirrel is like a coffee pot because of its shape.
2 __ The squirrel is like a coffee pot because both are cosy-looking but may in fact be dangerous.
3 __ The squirrel is a very well-behaved animal.
4 __ Grey squirrels eat the bark of trees and make them die.
5 __ People think that grey squirrels are lovable.
6 __ Grey squirrels eat red-brown nuts.
7 __ The squirrel is killed by the park keeper.
8 __ The keeper believes in Christian principles.
9 __ The squirrel is the keeper's friend.
10 __ Christians behave according to their beliefs.

Check with other groups. Have you all got the same answers? Look particularly at questions 9 and 10. If your answers are different, can you explain why?

Who do you think is worse: the keeper or the squirrel? Can you say why?

III The moral of the story

In small groups, try to decide upon a moral for this poem. Choose one of these or write your own:

People do the opposite of what they believe in.
Things are not what they seem.
Animals don't count.
Look after yourself – no one else will look after you.

Write your morals on the board. Can most people agree on one?

IV Problems

Work in a small group. Think of a problem. Choose an animal that you can link it with. Here are some examples to choose from, or think of your own.

avoiding problems – an ostrich with its head in the sand
forgetting your friend's birthday – an elephant
cheating – the fox
hiding things about yourself from people – a chameleon
working mothers – kangaroos
working too hard – ants
being lazy – lizards or sloths

Write a short paragraph using the animal to talk about the problem. Read it to others in the class.

Ku Klux

I Is there a link?

Work in groups of three. Look at these photographs. What could be the link between the two photographs? Imagine the situations before the moment when each photograph was taken.

II 'Man's inhumanity to man'

Here are eight possible reasons for the fact that people often behave cruelly to each other. They may help to explain violence in the world. In your groups, put these reasons in order, from the one which best explains violence to the one which least explains it.

People fear anything different from themselves.
People feel that people like themselves are superior to others.
People enjoy violence.
People are descended from animals, and animals are naturally cruel.
People have to protect their own situation and property.
People feel that their beliefs must be imposed at whatever cost.
People are treated badly in their families, and then are violent towards others when they grow up.
People feel that they are victims of society and must fight back.

Do most people in your class agree on the order to be chosen?

III A code for humane humans

With a partner, write a set of rules which could prevent people from treating other people inhumanely.
For example:

Treat others as you would like them to treat you.
Do not give way to anger.
Understand other people's points of view.

Show your code to other groups and try to establish an overall code for the class.

Ku Klux

They took me out
To some lonesome place.
They said: "Do you believe
In the great white race?"

I said, "Mister,   5
To tell you the truth,
I'd believe in anything
If you'd just turn me loose."

The white man said, "Boy,
Can it be   10
You're a-standin' there
A-sassin' me?"

They hit me in the head
And knocked me down.
And then they kicked me   15
On the ground.

A klansman said, "Nigger,
Look me in the face—
And tell me you believe in
The great white race."   20

Langston Hughes

IV Ku Klux

Before you listen to the poem, check that you understand the following words and expressions:

a lonesome place – a deserted place far from anywhere
to turn someone loose – to let them go, set them free
a-sassin' – 'to sass someone' in America means to be rude
a klansman – a member of the Ku Klux Klan
Nigger – a term of abuse used for black people

T Listen to the poem while you read it.

V Feelings

What are your feelings as you read this poem? Can you put them into words? Write them down for yourself.

VI A letter

Imagine that you saw a scene like the one in the poem. Write a letter to a close friend describing your experience.

World Geography and the Rainbow Alliance

I Essential ingredients

Here are some reasons that make you think you belong to a place. Tick [√] the ones that you think are essential.
You belong to a place when:

You belong to a place when :

you live where you were born.

you live where your family were born.

you have a right to vote.

you pay taxes and you own property.

you have citizenship or a passport.

your children were born there.

you have the same religion as people around you.

you talk the same language in your home as
    people outside.

people treat you as if you belong.

you approve of the government in power.

Find out what other people in your class think. What were the three reasons ticked most often? Discuss why these reasons are so important. If you use these three reasons, how many people in your class feel they belong to the place where they live?

World Geography and the Rainbow Alliance

Peking is in China
As Kingston is in Jamaica
As Delhi is in India
As nowhere do we belong
You and I.   *5*

And should we ever run away
Where shall we run to?
And should we ever fight a war,
Who shall we fight for?
You and I.   *10*

At the end of the rainbow
Is a country of goodness
If we form an alliance,
Will we ever be free
To belong?   *15*

Or shall we always be carrying
Our ancestors coffins in a bag?
Searching the globe
For a place to belong
You and I.   *20*

Meiling Jin

II Dream and reality

⊞ Listen to the poem while you read it.

There is a contrast in it between things that exist in the 'real' world and things that are in a 'dream' world of the future or the past.
Listen to the poem again. Do the following parts of the poem belong to either of the categories in the grid below?
Work with a partner and tick the appropriate column.

	World of reality	World of dreams
Kingston		
nowhere		
you		
should we ever		
where shall we		
rainbow		
at the end of the rainbow		
country of goodness		
alliance		
free		
ancestors coffins		
globe		
a place to belong		

Get together with another group. Have you all got the same answers? Which column did you tick for you? Who could you be? Did you tick different columns for rainbow and end of the rainbow?

With the other group, talk about the possible meanings of a rainbow. What do you think the metaphor ancestors coffins means? Does everyone in your group agree?

III Rainbow alliance

In a group of three or four, imagine that you are explorers who get to the end of the rainbow and find a country of goodness. Send home a short report for the Travel Page of your local newspaper. In it, tell your readers the name of the country and write about some of the following:

the political system (a democracy? a monarchy?)
family institutions (marriage? families?)
the way children are treated (before they go to school; kind of
  school . . . ?)
leisure activities
religious practices
the population (all the same race or multi-cultural . . . ?)
special features . . .

Talent and Performer

I Danger

Have you ever done anything that was very dangerous? In a small group, compare experiences. If you've never done anything dangerous, say what you would like to do or why you feel you could never do anything dangerous. What is the most dangerous thing that anyone in your class has ever done?

Talent

This is the word *tightrope*. Now imagine
a man, inching across it in the space
between our thoughts. He holds our breath.

There is no word *net*.

You want him to fall, don't you?
I guessed as much; he teeters but succeeds.   5
The word *applause* is written all over him.

Carol Ann Duffy

Performer

Tight-roper, care, do not look down,
Think of the thread beneath your foot,
Forget the pony and the clown,
Discard the circus, see before
Your gaze a safety held, complete   5

And, after that, the tidal roar

Of watchers, some of whom no doubt
Wanted a death. You have an hour
When you can cast your terror out,
Depend no more on balance but   10
On earth whose ground gives you the power,
To think, to snatch that rope and cut.

Elizabeth Jennings

II Two tightrope poems

T Listen to the two poems while you read them.

With a partner, find in the poems the words or expressions which refer to

1 walking on a rope
2 the height of the rope
3 protection for the walker
4 equilibrium
5 the walker's feelings
6 the audience's feelings

III A talented performer

What are the similarities and the differences between the two poems? Work in pairs. Talk about each one of these questions and jot down a few notes.

1 Who is the speaker talking to in each poem?
2 What is the tightrope image about in each poem?
3 Which of these elements is not common to both poems?

suspense	a safety net
balance	applause
a circus setting	the audience wanting an accident

4 Are the endings similar in both poems?

From your notes, give a summary of your discussion to the class.

Which poem do you prefer? Do most people agree?

IV Circus acts

Here is a list of some circus acts. Choose two or three of them and, with a partner, use them to talk about events in your daily life. For example:

Every time I talk with you I feel as if I'm putting my head in the lion's mouth.
Every time the teacher asks me questions I jump through hoops of fire.

performing bears
jugglers
lion tamers
tigers jumping through hoops of fire
fire eaters
trapeze artists
seals balancing balls on their noses
acrobats on horseback
clowns in exploding cars
motor cyclists on the wall of death
escape artists
sword swallowers
knife throwers

Join up with two other groups and write down some of your sentences to make a short poem. Begin each line with: 'Every time I . . . ' Read out your poem to the rest of the class.

Not Waving But Drowning

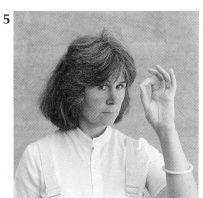

I What do you mean?

Work in small groups. What do these gestures mean? Do they
mean the same in all cultures?

Do you know any other gestures which can cause
misunderstandings in different cultures? What about
expressions and pronunciation?
In your group, build up a bank of gestures, expressions, or
pronunciations which can be misunderstood.

II Not Waving But Drowning

☐ Listen to the poem while you read it. Who says what?
Against each line, write:

n if the narrator of the poem is speaking
dm if the dead man is speaking
op if other people are speaking.
Check your answers with other groups.

Not Waving But Drowning

Nobody heard him, the dead man,
But still he lay moaning:
I was much further out than you thought
And not waving but drowning.

Poor chap, he always loved larking   5
And now he's dead
It must have been too cold for him his heart gave way,
They said.

Oh no no no, it was too cold always
(Still the dead one lay moaning)   10
I was much too far out all my life
And not waving but drowning.

Stevie Smith

III Moaning and larking

Draw a line to connect each one of the expressions on the left
with its meaning on the right:

moaning	familiar way of saying 'man'
larking	being far from shore/ being different or eccentric
heart gave way	making a sound of suffering or complaint
being too far out	having a good time
drowning	have a heart attack
chap	dying in water

IV Too far out

T Here are three people talking about things that happened to
them. Listen to each one and in a small group decide:

who they are talking about
what is unusual about the people being talked about
are they 'too far out'? In what ways?

In your group, can you think of any other situations where
there are people who could be described as 'too far out'?

V Misunderstandings

In your group, look back at your bank of possible
misunderstandings. Choose one of them and build up a sketch
about it. The sketch should contain at least three roles: the two
involved in the misunderstanding, and an observer. Perform
your sketch to the class.

Who Loves You

1 **Photos of loved ones**

Where do you keep photos of your loved ones?

In photograph albums
In your wallet
In a locket
Framed on your bedroom wall
Framed on your work desk
Nowhere – I don't believe in keeping photos
Other places: _____

With three or four other students, compare your answers. What happens when your loved ones are away from home? Do you tend to look at the photos more often? Do you put them in a more prominent place?

Who Loves You

I worry about you travelling in those mystical machines.
Every day people fall from the clouds, dead.
Breathe in and out and in and out easy.
Safety, safely, safe home.

Your photograph is in the fridge, smiles when the light comes on.   5
All the time people are burnt in the public places.
Rest where the cool trees drop to a gentle shade.
Safety, safely, safe home.

Don't lie down on the sands where the hole in the sky is.
Too many people being gnawed to shreds.   10
Send me your voice however it comes across oceans.
Safety, safely, safe home.

The loveless men and homeless boys are out there and angry.
Nightly people end their lives in the shortcut.
Walk in the light, steadily hurry towards me.   15
Safety, safely, safe home. (Who loves you?)
Safety, safely, safe home.

Carol Ann Duffy

II I worry about . . .

T Listen to the poem while you read it.

The person in the poem worries about the loved one in various far away situations. Match the dangers in the following list to the situations in the poem. Some of the dangers might fit more than one situation in the poem and one situation might have more than one danger.

fires in hotels
airplane travel
dangerous animals
attacks in dark alleyways in cities
the gap in the ozone layer
terrorist attacks

bombs in restaurants or shops
gangs of thugs
skin cancer from sunlight
muggings
pollution
disease

III How do you ward off danger?

When our loved ones are away, we sometimes try different ways of trying to keep danger away from them, or at least of stopping ourselves from worrying too much:
1 We talk to them – in our minds, on the telephone, or in letters – to tell them to be careful.
2 We use some form of calming routine – a form of prayer, or an invocation: a repetition of words, as though the words could have a magic power to ward off danger.

The poem has a pattern which shows both of these ways. Read the poem again, and with a partner write down the line numbers in which each one of these ways appears:

Way of warding off danger or preventing worry	lines
telling the loved one to be careful	3
a calming routine of repeated words	4

Compare your results with other people in the class. Do you have any special routines to help you calm your worries?

IV Breathe in and out

What recommendations would you like to make to a loved one who is away from home? Write a letter to that person. Begin:

I worry about you . . .

The Health-Food Diner

1 **Food**

Are there any foods that you don't eat? Why?
Are there foods that you eat or drink that you really consider unhealthy?

Work in a group of three. Imagine that you are leaving Earth in a spaceship. From now on you are going to have nothing but pills to eat. Tonight you are having your very last real meal. Your group can order any four courses that you like, with something to drink, but all three of you must have the same meal. Choose your menu.

Compare with others in your class.

The Health-Food Diner

No sprouted wheat and soya shoots
And Brussels in a cake,
Carrot straw and spinach raw,
(Today, I need a steak).

Not thick brown rice and rice pilau   5
Or mushrooms creamed on toast,
Turnips mashed and parsnips hashed,
(I'm dreaming of a roast).

Health-food folks around the world
Are thinned by anxious zeal,   10
They look for help in seafood kelp
(I count on breaded veal).

No Smoking signs, raw mustard greens,
Zucchini by the ton,
Uncooked kale and bodies frail   15
Are sure to make me run.

Loins of pork and chicken thighs
And standing rib, so prime,
Pork chops brown and fresh ground round
(I crave them all the time).   20

Irish stews and boiled corned beef
And hot dogs by the scores,
Or any place that saves a space
For smoking carnivores.

Maya Angelou

II Dinner at the Health-Food Diner

[T] Listen to the poem while you read it.

Work in small groups. In the poem, what are the names of these foods? Tick [√] the ones you could get at the health-food diner. A few of them have been done for you.

— pork roasts *loins of pork*
— white meat on a bone _____
— meat preserved by salt and cooked in water *boiled corn beef*
√ miniature vegetable marrows *zucchini*
— meat cooked in vegetables in a liquid _____
— a large piece of meat cooked in the oven _____
√ two leafy vegetables used in salads *mustard green* *kale*
— vegetables in a sauce _____
— a roast of beef with the bones still attached *standing rib*
— a seed with its outside covering still on, used as a main food in many eastern countries _____
√ two root vegetables *turnips* *parsnips*
— a thin slice of very young beef covered in crumbs and fried *breaded veal*
— seaweed _____
— minced beef *ground round*
— very thin slices of a raw orange vegetable _____
√ cereal plants that are beginning to sprout *sprouted wheat*
— sausage in a bun _____
— meat cut up into separate portions, still on the bone *pork chops*
— small round green vegetables cooked into a shape _____
— a slab of grilled red beef _____
√ the seed of a bean-type plant that is beginning to sprout *soya shoots*

What is the speaker's attitude to health food? What are the expressions which reveal it? Are you a 'herbivore' (a vegetarian) or 'carnivore' (a meat-eater)? Do you agree with the speaker? Do you find the poem amusing or irritating? Do you all have the same reaction?

III It's bad for you

Work in small groups. In three minutes only, write down all the things which are bad for you or which cause harm to others.

Choose one of them. In the first column write the remarks people make to defend it and in the second column write what people say to attack it. For example:

Smoking

Defence	Attack
It's my personal choice.	*You're polluting my air.*

IV Opposing views

In pairs, write a dialogue between two people who disagree about one of the topics. You can use some of the expressions you've listed. Act out your dialogue to another group.

The Telephone Call

1 Telephone calls

In a small group, compare your answers to these questions:

How many phone calls do you make in a week?
How long is your average phone call?
Do you always answer the phone?
Is the telephone something you couldn't live without, or a necessary evil?
What is your reaction to unwanted phone calls: selling, advertising, heavy breathers?
What do you do if you have an unwanted phone call?
Do you always expect the best or the worst when you pick up the telephone?

The Telephone Call

They asked me 'Are you sitting down?
Right? This is Universal Lotteries',
they said, 'You've won the top prize,
the Ultra-super Global Special.
What would you do with a million pounds?   5
Or, actually, with more than a million —
not that it makes a lot of difference
once you're a millionaire.' And they laughed.

'Are you OK?' they asked—'Still there?
Come on, now, tell us, how does it feel?'   10
I said 'I just . . . I can't believe it!'
They said 'That's what they all say.
What else? Go on, tell us about it.'
I said 'I feel the top of my head
has floated off, out through the window,   15
revolving like a flying saucer.'

'That's unusual' they said. 'Go on.'
I said 'I'm finding it hard to talk.
My throat's gone dry, my nose is tingling.
I think I'm going to sneeze—or cry.'   20
'That's right' they said, 'don't be ashamed
of giving way to your emotions.
It isn't every day you hear
you're going to get a million pounds.

Relax, now, have a little cry;   25
we'll give you a moment . . . ' 'Hang on!' I said.
'I haven't bought a lottery ticket
for years and years. And what did you say
the company's called?' They laughed again.
'Not to worry about a ticket.   30
We're Universal. We operate
a Retrospective Chances Module.

Nearly everyone's bought a ticket
in some lottery or another,
once at least. We buy up the files,   35
feed the names into our computer,
and see who the lucky person is.'
'Well, that's incredible' I said.
'It's marvellous. I still can't quite . . .
I'll believe it when I see the cheque.'   40

. . .

Fleur Adcock

II The Telephone Call

T Listen to the poem while you read it.

With another student, look at the graph below. The horizontal
line shows the lines in the poem where the speaker is
responding to the telephone call. The vertical line gives a scale
of emotions. Draw the line of the speaker's feelings as s/he
listens.

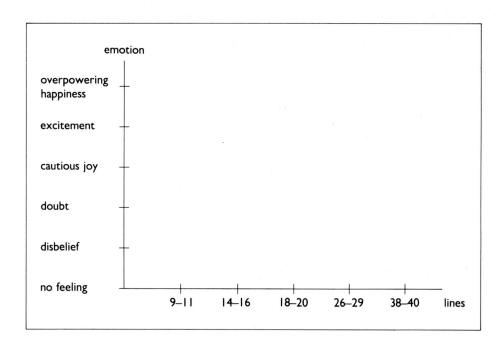

III Giving way to emotion

T Listen to the poem again.
Expressions like these probably helped you draw your graph:

Well, that's incredible
I feel the top of my head has floated off . . .
I think I'm going to cry
I can't believe it
My nose is tingling
I think I'm going to sneeze
I still can't quite believe it
I'm finding it hard to talk
It's marvellous
My throat's gone dry
I'll believe it when I see it

Work with a partner. List the expressions under the following headings:

Disbelief	*Physical signs of excitement*	*Overpowering happiness*

Compare with another group.

In your groups, discuss these questions:
What do you feel about giving way to emotion? Is it acceptable in your society?
Do men and women show emotion in the same way?
What is an acceptable way to show: happiness, love, anger, grief?

IV Endings

The last stanza of the poem is missing. With a partner, write the end of the conversation. Read out your endings to others and compare them.
T Listen to the end of the poem. How different is it from yours?
What do you feel about the ending? Surprised? Cross? Amused? Irritated? What do you think the speaker felt? Where would you place this reaction on the graph?

With a partner, imagine other prizes that Universal Lotteries could offer in the Lottery of Life.

V Dear Diary . . .

Imagine that you are the speaker. Write your diary entry for that evening.

Ballad of the Clairvoyant Widow

I Clairvoyance

Work in small groups. Imagine that you are sitting around a crystal ball and that you can see everything that is going on in your city. Make notes on what you see. Compare with others in your class.

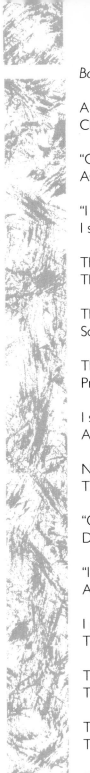

Ballad of the Clairvoyant Widow

A kindly Widow Lady, who lived upon the hill,
Climbed to her attic window and gazed across the sill.

"Oh tell me, Widow Lady, what is it that you see,
As you look across my city, in God's country?"

"I see ten million windows, I see ten thousand streets,   5
I see the traffic doing miraculous feats.

The lawyers all are cunning, the business men are fat,
Their wives go out on Sunday beneath the latest hat.

The kids play cops and robbers, the kids play mumbly-peg,
Some learn the art of thieving, and some grow up to beg;   10

The rich can play polo, the poor can do the shag,
Professors are condoning the cultural lag.

I see a banker's mansion with twenty wood-grate fires,
Alone, his wife is grieving for what her heart desires.

Next door there is a love-nest of plaster board and tin,   15
The rats soon will be leaving, the snow will come in."

"Clairvoyant Widow Lady with an eye like a telescope,
Do you see any sign or semblance of that thing called 'Hope'?"

"I see the river harbor, alive with men and ships,
A surgeon guides a scalpel with thumb and finger tips.   20

I see grandpa surviving a series of seven strokes,
The unemployed are telling stale unemployment jokes.

The gulls ride on the water, the gulls have come and gone,
The men on rail and roadway keep moving on and on.

The salmon climb the rivers, the rivers nudge the sea,   25
The green comes up for ever in the fields of our country."

Theodore Roethke

II   Ballad part 1

⊤ Listen to the first eight couplets of the poem while you read them.

Here is a list of things that the Widow Lady sees. With a partner, put them in the right order.
A children playing games
B university teachers explaining complicated things
C clever and possibly dishonest professional men
D rich and poor people at leisure
E an abandoned home which once had a happy couple in it
F an unsatisfied woman in a large rich house
G a busy street scene
H smartly dressed women

Check your answers with another pair.

III   Hope

⊤ Read and listen to the rest of the poem.
Are the things the Widow Lady sees hopeful or not? Write H (hopeful) or U (unhopeful) against each line. Do you agree with others in your class? If you have different letters, explain your choices.

IV   A ballad?

The ballad is a very old form of poetry and there are various kinds. However, they can all be sung and they all tell a story in verse. Does Roethke's poem fit into this category? In small groups, can you retell the story? Can anyone in your class set it to music?

V   Looking into the future

In a small group, look twenty years into the future and talk about what you see. What are the cities going to be like? What is the world going to be like? What kind of things will today's babies be doing then? Is your group optimistic or pessimistic? Make notes of your discussions. Then compare your ideas with other groups.

VI   The Clairvoyant Times

The Clairvoyant Times is offering a prize for the best or most amusing poem that tells a story about the future. Write a poem, by yourself or with a friend. Elect a panel of judges to read all the poems and choose three winners.

I **Legendary beasts**

Work with a partner. Match each beast with one of these
definitions. Which of the beasts exist only in mythology and
which do you find in the natural world?

an Arabian bird which sets fire to itself and rises again from the
   ashes every five hundred years
a bull-headed man living in a Cretan labyrinth and eating
   human flesh
a reptile which lives in fire
a white horse with one long horn on its forehead
a monster which looks like a reptile, has wings, and breathes
   fire
a sea creature with the tail of a fish and the front parts of a
   horse

Check your answers with others in the class. Imagine what
each beast can mean, for example a 'dragon' can mean a fierce
person in English-speaking countries. Does it have the same
connotations in your country? Do you know of any other
mythical beasts? What are their connotations?

'The fire in leaf and grass . . . '

The fire in leaf and grass
so green it seems
each summer the last summer.

The wind blowing, the leaves
shivering in the sun,   5
each day the last day.

A red salamander
so cold and so
easy to catch, dreamily

moves his delicate feet   10
and long tail. I hold
my hand open for him to go.

Each minute the last minute

Denise Levertov

II 'The fire in leaf and grass . . . '

T   Listen to the poem while you read it.

In small groups, think of several appropriate titles. Consider
particularly some of the poem's patterns, for example the
repetition of so: so green . . . so cold . . . so easy to catch; the move
from each summer to each day to each minute; the contrast between
heat and cold.

Join up with another group and decide on the best title.

Your teacher will tell you the poet's title. Do you prefer your
group's title?

III Moments

Think of a special moment in your life, when time seemed to
stand still. Write a short poem describing that moment. You
can use the following pattern if you like:

My _____

On the _____

More than _____

Every _____

New _____

To _____

So _____

Teacher's Notes on Individual Poems

Unusual vocabulary is glossed at the beginning of the notes on each individual poem. A (●) indicates words that might be useful to learn and that could therefore be pre-taught.

happiness ——————————— 6

This poem celebrates the happiness to be found in an everyday, cosy, domestic situation. It has an innovative form, typical of this Liverpool poet's work.

vocabulary gloss

●	a bottle	a baby's bottle
●	cot	a baby's bed
	fella	phonetic rendering of the normal spelling, fellow
	littlefella	a small boy
	outsings	the poet's way of saying sings louder than

I The aim of this activity is to introduce the theme of small things which can produce happiness. Asking students to agree on the two most important items is designed to stimulate discussion. There is obviously no right or wrong answer, and final agreement is not necessary or desirable. It is often useful to have a general class feedback before going on to the next section.

II ⊤ Answers
1 The person in the poem is not alone.
2 The leaves on the trees have not begun to fall yet (the trees are none the worse for Autumn, that is, they still have all their leaves, even though it is Autumn.)
3 The bottle is for the baby (the littlefella).
4 One person stays in bed comfortably, stretching out into the warm space left when the other got up.
5 The baby is awake (and singing!).
6 There is no single right answer to this question. Poetry often offers multiple levels of meaning. Both these sentences can be 'true': the first one could be said to be a literal interpretation of the poem, the second a metaphorical one. If necessary, this may be the moment to introduce learners to the concept of metaphor.

The object of the rewriting exercise is not to 'ruin' the poem, but to make students see what the poem is doing and why.

If learners have difficulty talking about the effects of the way the poem is set out, you could ask questions like:
Do you feel this poem is formal or informal? Is it cosy and intimate or cold and distant?
Look at the words that run together. Does this give you the feeling of immediacy? Rapidity? Something that is happening now? Something a bit surprising? Does it make the poem sound like words that a person is speaking?
Do the actions in the poem seem separate, or linked together? What about the people and their surroundings? Are they linked like the words? What about the separation of the last word (alone on its line). Does this give it special importance?

III Encourage students to read out their sentences to several people in the class.

Salad Poem ———————————— 8

A poem about the way in which both poets and painters intensify experience and revel in it.

vocabulary gloss

●	crisp	fresh, firm, brittle
	radish	small red and white vegetable eaten raw

I This is a guided fantasy to set the scene for the poem. Make sure that students are in a relaxed frame of mind before you start. If it's possible, put on a piece of soft, relaxing music. This can help to stimulate the imagination. Give the instructions in a smooth and soothing voice. Keep on asking questions about the mind painting (there are more questions in the pairwork activity) until you see that they are actually imagining their pictures.

II ⊤ Gentle Rousseau might be a reference not only to Henri Rousseau but also to nature-loving Jean-Jacques Rousseau.

The questionnaire is a framework for discussion. Not all the answers will be known, but it is a way of providing information and getting students to talk.

Questionnaire answers
1 a customs officer
2 naïve paintings with brilliant colours
3 an eighteenth-century philosopher
4 a plate of cold food
5 an English hymn. The words of the refrain are:
  All things bright and beautiful,
  All creatures great and small,
  All things wise and wonderful,
  The Lord God made them all.
6 All creatures great and small.
7 All three are correct.

48

III This is a framework for discussion. All the reasons could arguably be right. Encourage students to think of other painters who have a bright, colourful style. Students may or may not recognize Rousseau's style in the picture on the cover of this book.

IV If your students are short of ideas, write the names of a few people who are well-known celebrities on the blackboard. For example, with students in the UK and France, we have used: Dear Simone (de Beauvoir), Dear Nelson (Mandela), Dear Marie (Curie), Dear Florence (Nightingale), Dear Albert (Einstein), Dear Isaac (Newton), Dear Indira (Gandhi).

Classifying ——————————— 11

This poem explores the way in which individuals are unique, yet belong to general categories. Some teachers feel that this is a young person's poem, but we have used it successfully with adults as well. It works very successfully with groups of students who know each other well.

vocabulary gloss

- freckles small spots on the face brought out by the sun
  Guides a youth group for girls
  Recorders a group of people who play recorders (a flute-like musical instrument)
  fits in most things goes into most categories
  netball a game like basket ball played by girls in Britain
  jolly cheerful
- chat an informal conversation
  penny whistle a small tin flute

I Other categories could include, for example: plump/slim; tall/short; people who like reading/people who prefer television; people who always read an evening paper/people who never read an evening paper; people who wear watches or jewellery/people who never wear them; people who prefer formal clothes/people who like informal clothes; people who wear bright colours/people who prefer dark colours. Circulate among the groups and help students if they need it. At the end, ask groups to report back to the class so that there is a general feedback.

II ⊤ This is the drawing provided by the author.

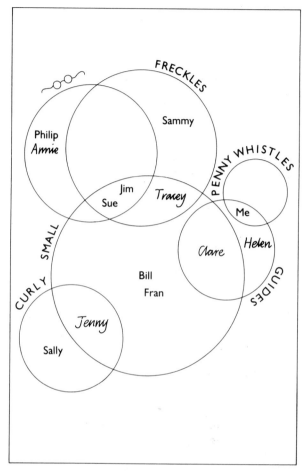

Categories not included on the diagram: boys' group, tall, recorders, football, girls, blonde, dark, netball, writing, maths, dislikes work, jolly, good for quiet chats, likes joking, plays the piano. Accept all reasons – but clearly the diagram is complicated enough as it is!

III The aim of drawing the diagram is to help students understand the main point of the poem i.e. that people share some characteristics with others but in some ways they are unique. It may be impossible to do it completely, so do not let the activity go on too long.
Suggestions for categorizing people: good/bad; black/white; religious/not religious; extrovert/introvert.

IV Encourage students to choose characteristics that are as ordinary as possible. Allow students to mingle until they find the person whose card they have. If some students find their person quickly, they can talk about the characteristics on the card.

A beautifully understated poem about coping with unwanted advice. The vocabulary is simple and should be known to most students.

I [T] Stop the tape before final stanza. The I in the poem could be anyone who is receiving advice: a child, a spouse, a friend.
The you in the poem is someone close to that person, who 'means well' (that is, has the person's interests at heart) and feels he or she can give advice. The relationship can be interpreted in different ways, but 'friendly' is probably too weak, and 'hostile' is probably too strong.

II [T] This is the last stanza.

Can we talk about it
and come up with something better
than either your or my opinion?

Play the last stanza to the students and allow time for discussion about the new direction the poem takes in this last stanza. To help discussion, you can ask questions like: Is there hope in this relationship? What future does it have? How should the two people behave to improve their relationship?
The whole poem is printed on page 60, and is repeated without a break on the tape.

III Suggested remarks to help students if necessary:
'When you're my age, you'll understand these things better.'
'I really think you're making a big mistake.'
'Don't forget I have a lot more experience.'
'You'll be sorry later.'
If time is short, students can write the reply for homework.

IV This follow-up activity can be done in a subsequent class if necessary. Encourage students to skim through the list of situations and choose one quickly. Some of them may be more suitable for your particular class than others.

It is sometimes better to limit preparation time, otherwise some groups never want to finish. We suggest ten minutes' preparation and ten minutes' acting time, but this will obviously vary with the level of the class.

Occasionally, monolingual classes slip into their native language during the preparation phase. We like to circulate and remind learners to use English as much as possible, but we do not worry unduly about temporary lapses. The role play will eventually be done in English. If it is appropriate in your circumstances, you might like to ask one or two of the groups to perform their role play as a sketch in front of the whole class.

We would like to thank Mike Beaumont for introducing us to this poem.

This poem raises the issue of the contrast between what elderly people think of themselves, and the way they are perceived by others.

vocabulary gloss

sack	a large shapeless bag
chattering	talking in a lively way
● sympathy	feeling sorry for somebody
● otherwise	if not
● do without	manage without something
● stiff	difficult to move (in this context)
rocking chair	a chair with its legs on curved rockers (see picture), often symbolizes old age
● stumble	walk unsteadily
study	stare (in this context)
● lungs	part of the body used for breathing
wind	breath (in this context)

I The aim of the questionnaire is to explore opinions and feelings about old age. There are no right or wrong answers. Encourage students to imagine each situation as it would be in their own country and compare.

II [T] This makes the students think about the poem and also functions as an overall comprehension exercise. At the end of the exercise ask students if there are any words in the poem that they still do not know. Get the class as a whole to guess from the context.
Suggested answers for sentence endings:

Column 1
likes to spend a quiet time thinking
is tired but hasn't given up
wants to be independent
hasn't changed inside
is very determined
is happy to be alive

Column 2
likes to hear people talking
seems quiet and must be sad
doesn't want to do anything any more
is nearing death
The following could go in both columns, and students should be encouraged to say why:
is slow and not too energetic
is full of aches and pains (the speaker's view of these may be less negative than other people's)
is lonely (the speaker denies this, but what are the undertones of the simile like a sack left on a shelf? Could this not denote loneliness?)

III Although the author is a black American woman, the speaker in the poem could be a man or a woman. Different readers visualize the speaker in different ways and express a preference for either the male voice or the female voice.

Expressions that could indicate that a black American is speaking:
Don't bring me no rocking chair (double negation, spoken language – the image of old people in rocking chairs on their porches also conjures up the Southern States in the USA); 'Cause tired don't mean lazy (verb form: 'don't' for 'doesn't' in spoken language); every goodbye ain't gone (contracted verb form: 'ain't')
Many of these expressions are also used in other regional forms of English.

IV If necessary, help the students individually with questions, to encourage diversity. Some examples are:
What does it feel like to be 100 years old?
Why do you think you have been able to live to this great age?
What is your first memory?
What is the most memorable event in your life?
What is the greatest change that has happened in your lifetime?

V If time is short, this can be done for homework. Many students do have their own recording equipment nowadays. Learners are sometimes reticent when asked to record themselves, but once convinced, they often enjoy the experience. Encourage students to read each other's articles, or listen to each other's tapes.

poem about the sun slinking off and pinning up a notice ——————— 18

With its interesting shape, this poem light-heartedly evokes a natural occurrence which happens daily but is nevertheless unexpected. Difficult or unusual vocabulary is dealt with in Section II.

I If your classroom has no window, ask your students to imagine the view through the window in the picture.

II T Answers 1–f, 2–c, 3–a, 4–h, 5–d, 6–g, 7–e, 8–b

III Answers a–2, b–4, c–1, d–5, e–3

Suggestions for other situations: high winds and waves indicating a hurricane coming; a hot muggy spell indicating rain; fields of cut hay indicating harvesting/autumn coming; dust on the horizon indicating a plague of locusts/wind storms

IV The shape of the poem: the spaces in the first stanza may suggest a contrast between stability and change; the sloping words may suggest the sun going down; the word moon, centred in capitals, may suggest a notice.

Reassure students that in writing their own short poem, there is no need to worry about rhyme. If necessary, help students with ideas, by suggesting a tree, a plant, a flower, rain, etc.

For a Five-Year-Old ——————————— 20
A caring relationship between a mother and her child turns out to have a dark side to it.

vocabulary gloss
- squash   kill by walking on
- trapped   caught
  purveyed   communicated
- harshest   difficult and unpleasant to hear

I A warm-up to explore the students' relationships to creepy crawlies. Groups report back any extreme reactions.

II T This activity helps comprehension of the poem and prepares the students for the contrast of the second stanza. Stop the tape at the end of the first stanza. Let students read/listen to it several times.

Possible answers
It's important to protect life, however small.
You should be kind to animals.
Children must learn from what parents tell them.
We should be careful not to destroy the natural world, even by accident.

III Answers
a kind of faith prevails — I have done wrong to members of our family.
your gentleness is moulded still by words from me — I told people things that were true but unpleasant.
me who drowned your kittens — You believe what I say.
me who betrayed your closest relatives — I killed your pets.
me who purveyed the harshest kind of truth to many another — You are kind because I tell you to be kind.

IV T Here is the tapescript:
My parents were always quarrelling and always telling my brother and me not to quarrel.
My parents smoked, but they were horrified when my sister started smoking.
My mother was always going on about my untidy room, but you should have seen our kitchen.

Fire and Ice ——————————————— 22
A compact and witty exploration of contrasting emotions.

vocabulary gloss

taste of	to sample; to have a brief experience of something
hold with	agree
perish	die
know enough of	know enough about something
suffice	be enough

I The aim of the warm-up activity is to familiarize students with some of the symbolic connotations of fire and ice.

II [T] Some of the statements refer to precise parts of the poem, while others refer to several.

1 From what I've tasted of desire/I hold with those who favor fire

  The speaker associates desire or passion with fire because of their destructive power.

2 I know enough of hate/To say that for destruction ice/Is also great

  Hatred is associated with ice.

3 Some say in ice.

4 The speaker favors fire while ice, though also great, would suffice

  Ice is enough but fire is favored over it.

5 From what I've tasted of desire/I hold with those who favor fire

  Desire destroys completely like fire.

6 I know of, i.e. he has observed it.

7 Some say the world will end in fire

8 The crucial words here are tasted of, i.e. has known something of.

III This activity can be done as follow-up immediately, or in a subsequent lesson. Preparation time will vary according to the level of the class, but ten to fifteen minutes should suffice. With more advanced classes, insist on the formal register suitable to a trial, and help students with this if necessary. The presentation phase will be more enjoyable if the roles have been distributed evenly throughout the class.

Love Letter ——————— 24

An interesting new political slant on a traditional theme.

vocabulary gloss

- jar   clear glass container
  well   a shaft dug in the ground where water is found

I [T] Here is the tapescript of the main points in the story of Samson and Delilah, from the Bible (Judges 14, 15 and 16).

Long ago there were two nations who were at war for many, many years, the Israelites and the Philistines. One of the leaders of the Israelites was a very strong man called Samson. He was so strong that he killed thousands of Philistines and burnt their crops. The Philistines found it impossible to capture him because of his great strength. Once they tried to imprison him in one of their cities but in the middle of the night he removed the gates of the city and went away with them on his back.

Although the Philistines were his enemies, Samson loved a Philistine woman called Delilah. The Philistines came to see Delilah and promised to give her eleven hundred pieces of silver if she found out the secret of Samson's great strength.

Three times Samson told her lies about his secret. Each time the Philistines tried to capture him, but could not. Delilah kept on asking and asking him. In the end he told her the truth: he would only be strong if he never cut his hair. While he was sleeping, Delilah cut his hair off, and his strength left him.

The Philistines were then able to capture him. They blinded him and imprisoned him. Some time later, they had a big feast to which they brought their prisoner to laugh at him. All the Philistine leaders were at the feast and there were many thousands of men and women watching from the roof of the temple. Samson asked them to place him between the two central pillars. His hair had now grown back again and his strength had returned. He pulled the temple down on top of himself and all the Philistines.

II [T] The questions are designed to elicit discussion of the poem and there are no right answers. Encourage the students to use the poem to justify their answers.

You can point out I been thinkin'/over what I done as an example of colloquial speech.

III The discussion in this activity is more important than final consensus. At the end, ask the groups to report back to the whole class.

IV If students need ideas, suggest other stories from the Bible, mythology, national history, fiction or films. Ask students to write up the stories for homework. If you have access to duplicating facilities, you or the students can make a class book of all the stories.

The Grey Squirrel ——————— 26

A witty, tightly-constructed and rather cynical comment on the mores of humans and animals.

vocabulary gloss

Grey squirrels are much more destructive than their red-brown cousins, red squirrels – if necessary, make sure students know that grey squirrels seriously damage trees by eating the bark and are considered pests in some parts of the world.

keeper   an official who looks after a park

I This exercise, which is intended to be done in a light-hearted manner, aims to familiarize students with the concept of the possibly deceptive nature of beautiful objects.
Answers
All the items can cause severe injury.
parcel – can contain a bomb
coffee pot – can contain very hot liquid
mushroom – can be poisonous
umbrella – can poke your eye out

polar bear – can maul you to death
mountain – can let you fall to your death, can
             cause you to die of cold, can make
             breathing difficult
hot air balloon – can let you fall to your death,
                can make breathing difficult,
                can cause you to die of cold

II [T] The aim is to help students with basic comprehension and also appreciation of the poem's irony. Encourage students to justify their answers by referring back to the poem.

Answers 1–S, 2–S, 3–D, 4–S, 5–D, 6–D, 7–S, 8–S, 9 – this is the literal meaning of the poem, but it is undermined by the irony of the keeper's actions; *10* – the poem says that the keeper, being a Christian, loves his enemies (and therefore behaves according to his principles), but once again the opposite is implied through irony.

III The morals stimulate discussion about the poem and its meaning. There is no right answer and different morals should be accepted if students can justify them.

IV Can be done as homework.

Ku Klux ———————————— 28

A powerful indictment of racial violence, written by a black American. Students are given help with potentially difficult vocabulary in Section IV.

I The Ku Klux Klan is a secret organization of white Protestant Americans, mainly in the South of the U.S.A., who use violence against blacks. They often cover themselves with sheets so that they remain anonymous when they commit acts of violence. There is thus a physical link between the pictures: the sheets worn by the Ku Klux Klan, and the sheet which traditionally covers dead bodies. In one case the sheet is covering the killer, in the other the killed. There are other metaphorical links: violence, human cruelty and death.

II The title of this activity comes from Robert Burns' poem *Man was made to mourn*.
These reasons provide a framework for discussion. Students will obviously disagree. There is no right or wrong grading.

III Ask students to write their code on the blackboard to make it easier to compare and select.

IV [T] Because the poem is so powerful and serious, we believe that silent reading and listening are the most appropriate.

V It is important to let students react individually. They are simply asked to jot down their own personal response as a fluency activity.

They should be allowed to keep their notes to themselves.

VI This writing activity could be done for homework.

World Geography and the Rainbow Alliance ———————————— 30

In a world of increasing migration, the poem addresses the question of rootlessness, establishing a contrast between present-day reality and an imagined ideal.

vocabulary gloss

should we ever fight	if we ever fought
alliance	an association, a formal grouping
ancestors	the people who lived before us
coffin(s)	a wooden box in which dead people are buried
globe	the Earth

I Allow enough time so that students can move informally around the class finding out what other people think. Then organize a class feedback. Nominate one or two students to ask the class how many people ticked each reason and record the scores. Allow time for a final class discussion on people's feelings about where they belong.

II [T] The grid is a framework for discussion, and the students may come up with different answers. However, check that they are aware of the fact that should we ever signals a hypothesis. You and I signals that the speaker, though in exile, is not totally alone.
Rainbow may have different connotations in different countries. In English, it usually evokes happiness or better times to come. At the end of the rainbow there is said to be a pot of gold that no one ever attains. Since it contains the whole spectrum of colours, a rainbow is also used to describe multi-faceted things.
ancestors coffins is written in the poem without an apostrophe. The metaphor is open to interpretation but obviously carries some connotation of inherited customs, etc.
Check that the students understand how a metaphor works.

III Students enjoy reading each other's reports. If possible, pin them up on the classroom wall.

Talent and Performer ———————————— 32

Two metaphorical poems about tightrope-walking. Although they are conceptually more difficult than some other poems in this anthology, with a fairly heavy vocabulary load, the contextualization of the theme and the contrast between the two make them accessible to most students at this level.

vocabulary gloss

tightrope	a stretched rope on which somebody walks, for example in a circus
inching across	moving very slowly and carefully, inch by inch
● to hold your breath	to stop breathing because of suspense
● net	a device to catch an acrobat who falls off the tightrope
teeters	almost falls
thread	fine rope (in this context)
pony	small horse
● discard	forget (in this context)
safety	a protective net (in this context)
tidal roar	a sound that rises and falls like the sea (in this context)
cast out	throw out, get rid of
● snatch	to seize, to catch

Sections II and III are designed to provide help and support with some of this vocabulary.

I A warm-up for the connotations of danger in the tightrope image. Ask students to report back to the whole class on particularly dangerous or memorable experiences.

II ⊤ Students will need to listen to and read the poem several times. You may like to use the following alternative procedure: divide the class into two groups, A and B; give group A one poem and group B the other; ask them to do the activity in pairs; then join up an A pair with a B pair to complete the activity and compare the poems.

Answers
1 inching; teeters; thread beneath your foot
2 in the space; to fall; do not look down; depend no more on balance but/On earth
3 net; safety held, complete
4 teeters; balance
5 **during the performance:** Think of the thread beneath your foot (**concentration**); care, Forget the pony . . . , see before/Your gaze . . . (**fear, concentration**)
afterwards: The word applause is written all over him, the tidal roar of watchers (**satisfaction**); you can cast your terror out (**relief**)
6 He holds our breath (**suspense**); You want him to fall, don't you?, some of whom no doubt/Wanted a death . . . (**desire for a spectacular accident**); the word *applause* . . . , the tidal roar of watchers (**enthusiasm, approval of the feat accomplished**)

III Answers
1 In *Talent*, not to the tightrope walker but to somebody else.
In *Performer*, to the tightrope walker.
2 In *Talent*, a possible interpretation is a situation of communication and the tightrope is a metaphor for that communication. In *Performer*, the image is more straightforward but more open-ended. It could be, for example, a metaphor for dangerous situations in life.
3 a circus setting
4 No. *Talent* ends with the applause, while *Performer* goes on to explore the tightrope walker's feelings after the event.

After they have discussed these four questions, pairs can be asked to report some of the main points to the class.

The final question in this activity ('Which poem do you prefer?') is deceptively simple. It can be done as part of the pairwork or as general class feedback. It usually generates a lot of discussion and deeper levels of understanding of the two poems.

IV If it is useful, you can discuss the difference between simile, as in the first example, and metaphor, as in the second example, and encourage them to be aware of the difference in their own sentences.

Not Waving But Drowning ——————— 34

A witty but rather grim vignette which depends on a play with the two meanings of the expression 'far out'.
Difficult vocabulary is dealt with in Section III.

I This warm-up activity is designed to sensitize students to the possibility of communication being misunderstood.
The gestures mean:
1 in many countries, for example Spain: eating; in others, for example Italy: precise, salutation
2 in many countries: victory or peace
3 in Spain: You rotten sponger; in Greece: You'd better watch it; in Malta: You are a sneaky little so-and-so; in Italy: Get lost; in Portugal: How wonderful
4 in Saudi Arabia: an insult; in Italy or South America: a compliment; in France: disbelief
5 in north America: A-O.K.; in France: zero; in Japan: money; in Tunisia: a threat to kill
6 in Italy: good or lots; in other countries: a query or emphasis

II ⊤ This activity helps comprehension but also makes students aware of the narrative voice in the poem.
Answers Line: 1–n, 2–n, 3–dm, 4–dm, 5–op, 6–op, 7–op, 8–n, 9–dm, 10–n, 11–dm, 12–dm

III Answers

moaning — making a sound of suffering or complaint
larking — having a good time
heart gave way — have a heart attack
being too far out — being far from shore/ being different or eccentric
drowning — dying in water
chap — familiar way of saying 'man'

IV T Accept all reasonable comments.

Here is the tapescript of the conversations:

1 *I went to this party, you know, and I met Bob Smith, that amazing theatre director . . . everybody's heard of him. He went round kissing everybody . . . and you wouldn't believe how he was dressed. He had those Arabian slippers, you know, with turned up toes, with sequins on them . . . it was just so far out, and . . .*

2 *I was coming home last night and as I walked over the bridge I saw this couple and they had this sign up saying, 'Homeless, Please help', and they had a baby, and a dog with them as well . . .*

3 *You know when I was on holiday last year, I was outside the station and this man walked up leading a horse with his baggage on the back, all tied up with string, and he had, you know, long hair, and his clothes were rather strange . . . And we got talking and he told me he was following in the footsteps of a famous gypsy leader of the nineteenth century . . .*

V Can be done in a subsequent lesson. Circulate and help students.

Who Loves You ———————— 36

A poem which will touch a nerve in anyone who has ever worried about far away loved ones. Its skilful blend of meditation and exhortation follows the rhythms of an anxious mind, punctuated by an incantatory refrain to ward off danger.

vocabulary gloss

mystical machines	the poet's metaphor for aeroplanes
gnaw	bite at or chew constantly, so as to cause gradual wearing away
shreds	small pieces, strips

I This warm-up exercise focuses upon the idea of photographs to remind us of our loved ones when they are away.

II T Possible answers
fires in hotels – line 6
aeroplane travel – line 2
dangerous animals – line 10
attacks in dark alleyways in cities – lines 13 and 14
the gap in the ozone layer – line 9
terrorist attacks – lines 2, 6, 10 and 14
bombs in restaurants or shops – line 6
gangs of thugs – line 13
skin cancer from sunlight – line 9
muggings – lines 13 and 14
pollution – lines 9 and 10
disease – line 10

You may want to draw students' attention to the contrast between heat/danger (people burnt) and cold/safety (the cold fridge, the cool trees).
Telling the loved one to be careful: lines 3, 7, 11, 15 (the third line in each stanza).
A calming routine: lines 4, 8, 12, 16, 17 (the last line in the first three stanzas, the last line repeated in the final stanza, rather in the form of a refrain).
The aim of the activity is to encourage students to read the poem again to appreciate its highly patterned form.

IV Students who find writing difficult can be told to look once again at the list of dangers in Section II: which of these do they find most threatening? They can then write a very short letter telling the loved one to beware of that particular danger.

The Health-Food Diner ———————— 38

The unexpected rhymes and racy rhythm make this poem an amusing comment on vegetarian habits or fads.

vocabulary gloss

Although this poem looks as if it may have a heavy vocabulary load, most of the difficulties are to do with the names of unknown foods. Much of this does not need to be learnt. Section II presents the food words within a problem-solving context, but you may wish to ensure that the students also understand the following:

zeal	enthusiasm	carnivores	meat eaters
frail	weak	by the score	in large numbers
crave	want very much		(in this context)

I This activity offers a stimulus for discussion. The discussion is more important than the final decision.

II T Answers
white meat on a bone – chicken thigh
meat cooked in vegetables in a liquid – Irish stews
a large piece of meat cooked in the oven – a roast
√ vegetables in a sauce – mushrooms creamed on toast
√ a seed with its outside covering still on, used as main food in many eastern countries – rice
√ seaweed – seafood kelp
√ very thin slices of raw orange vegetable – carrot straw
sausage in a bun – hot dog
√ small round green vegetables cooked into a shape – Brussels in a cake
a slab of grilled red beef – a steak

In the poem, meat is considered as rather unhealthy food. The speaker describes people who eat health food as looking thin, weak (bodies frail) and neurotic (anxious zeal).

III The three-minute time limit helps to make this activity more game-like. It is useful to have a timer. Other examples of things that are bad for you or which cause harm to others: alcohol, chocolates, the exhaust from cars, smoke from coal fires, smoke from factories, nuclear energy.

IV As a final feedback, one or two groups can act out their dialogues to the whole class.

The Telephone Call ——————— 40

A narrative poem with an unexpected twist at the end.

vocabulary gloss

● lotteries	a lottery is a game of chance in which you buy a ticket and can win a prize
ultra-super Global special	a very special prize
floated off	flew gently away
revolving	turning
flying saucer	a spaceship from outer space
● tingling	a funny nervous feeling
● don't be ashamed	don't feel bad (in this context)
● hang on	wait
Retrospective Chances Module	a kind of lottery which you can win a long time after buying a ticket
files	records
the line went dead	the other person put the phone down

I A general stimulus for discussion to set the scene.

II T Stop the cassette before the final stanza. Ensure that the students record the disbelief that the speaker expresses in lines 9–11 through silence, and the dip in belief in lines 26–29, when the speaker remembers that s/he hasn't bought a lottery ticket for years. A possible line showing the speaker's feelings is shown below.

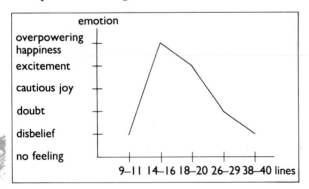

III T For advanced students: it may be useful for them to listen once again to the poem and mark in the most important stresses, as well as rising or falling intonation. This will help them to see how the intonation pattern expresses emotion. Here are possible answers within the context of the poem. The same expressions could be used for different emotions with other intonation patterns.

Well, that's incredible (overpowering happiness)
I feel the top of my head has floated off . . . (overpowering happiness)
I think I'm going to cry (physical signs of excitement)
I can't believe it (disbelief)
My nose is tingling (physical signs of excitement)
I think I'm going to sneeze (physical signs of excitement)
I still can't quite believe it (disbelief)
I'm finding it hard to talk (physical signs of excitement)
It's marvellous (overpowering happiness)
My throat's gone dry (physical signs of excitement)
I'll believe it when I see it (disbelief)

IV T This is a prediction exercise where students can see that a variety of different endings were possible, so that they appreciate how unexpected the poem's is.
Here is the final stanza. The whole poem is printed on page 60, and repeated without a break on the tape.

'Oh,' they said. 'there's no cheque.'
'But the money?' 'We don't deal in money.
Experiences are what we deal in.
You've had a great experience, right?
Exciting? Something you'll remember?
That's your prize. So congratulations
from all of us at Universal.
Have a nice day!' And the line went dead.

Further class discussion could centre on practical jokes, especially by telephone — are they always wonderful experiences?

V This writing activity can be done for homework.

Ballad of the Clairvoyant Widow ——— 43

A modern witty reworking of a very old form, the ballad.

vocabulary gloss

clairvoyant	a person who has the power to see the future and other things that are usually invisible
● widow	a woman whose husband has died
● attic	small room at the top of a house

● gazed	took a long look
sill	the edge of the window
● feats	extraordinary actions
● cunning	clever and tricky
cops and robbers	a child's game
mumbly peg	a child's game played with a knife
● beg	to ask for money
polo	a game played on horseback, popular with rich people
the shag	a dance popular with poor people in the 1930s
condoning	approving of, not condemning
cultural lag	cultural differences
● mansion	very large house
wood-grate fires	open wood fires
● grieving	very sad
love-nest	a small cosy home for lovers
plaster board and tin	thin, flimsy building materials
● telescope	an instrument to help people see a long way off
semblance	something that looks like
● harbor	safe port for ships
● surgeon	a doctor who operates on people or cuts them open
scalpel	a sharp knife used by a surgeon
● strokes	severe and sometimes fatal attacks of illness in the brain
● stale	old
● gulls	sea birds
● salmon	type of fish
nudge	come into contact with (in this context)

I Make sure that students understand the meaning of clairvoyance: the alleged power of perceiving things beyond the natural range of the senses. Some clairvoyants use a crystal ball to help them see.

II [T] This is a point where pre-teaching of possible lexical difficulties might be useful. *Answers* 1– G lines 5, 6; 2–C line 7; 3– H line 8; 4– A line 9; 5– D line 11; 6– B line 12; 7– F lines 13, 14; 8– E lines 15, 16

III There may be disagreement about whether the lines in this section are hopeful or not, but the shift from human situations to the natural world might imply that survival of some kind is all that can be hoped for.

IV Students could be asked whether they know of any ballads in their own language. The main features of the ballad that need to be stressed here are the narrative element and the fact that it is sometimes set to music.

V Students are asked to make notes of the discussion in their original groups. New groups can then be formed, incorporating one student

from each one of the original groups. If there is time, a general class feedback can follow.

VI Remind students that their poems do not have to rhyme, but should have the narrative element that is a main feature of ballads. If students are musical at all, they might like to write songs and sing them. A prize, however small, always provides a good incentive.

'The fire in leaf and grass . . . ' ———— 46

A lyrical poem about an intense moment of existence when time seems to stand still.

vocabulary gloss

shivering	a small trembling movement
salamander	a lizard/a mythical creature that lives in fire

I By exploring mythical beasts and their connotations, this warm-up activity helps to sensitize students to the symbolic meanings that metaphors can convey. The double connotations of the salamander, the cold of the reptile and the fire of the mythological creature, provide one of the key patterns of the poem. Help students with the word 'connotation', if necessary. Here are the creatures with their definitions and possible connotations:

salamander – a real lizard or a mythological reptile which lives in fire (possible connotations: rapidity, intensity, durability)

phoenix – a mythological Arabian bird which sets fire to itself and rises again from the ashes every five hundred years (possible connotations: a person or thing of surpassing beauty or quality; renewal)

dragon – a mythological monster which looks like a reptile, has wings and breathes fire (possible connotations: fierceness, in some cultures leadership, superiority)

unicorn – a mythological white horse with one long horn on its forehead (possible connotations: unique quality, elegance)

a sea horse – a sea creature with the tail of a fish and the front parts of a horse, both mythological and real (possible connotations: elegance, rapidity)

Minotaur – a mythological bull-headed man living in a Cretan labyrinth and eating human flesh (possible connotation: danger)

II [T] The title of the poem is Living. It is printed with the title on page 60 and is read a second time on the tape preceded by the real title. The various stages of this activity are designed to get the students to explore the meaning of the poem through its literary patterns.

III Many students find this kind of stimulus helpful. If it is too constraining, allow students to choose their own forms.

The Poets

Fleur Adcock
Born in 1934 in Papa Kura on New Zealand's North Island, Fleur Adcock was educated in Wellington, where she obtained an M.A. from Victoria University. After briefly working as an assistant in Classics at the University of Otago, she held various library posts in New Zealand and Britain. She has lived in England since 1963. Her *Selected Poems* were published by Oxford University Press in 1983.

Maya Angelou
Born in St. Louis, Missouri, in 1928, Maya Angelou spent many of her childhood years in Stamps, Arkansas. She has been a singer, actress, dancer, black activist, editor as well as mother. *I Know Why the Caged Bird Sings*, the first of her volumes of autobiography, brought her celebrity.

Carol Ann Duffy
Born in Glasgow in 1955, Carol Ann Duffy moved to Staffordshire as a child. She took a degree in philosophy at the University of Liverpool in 1977. She works as a free-lance writer and lives in London.

Robert Frost
Born in 1874 in San Francisco, Robert Frost returned to his family's native New England in 1885. After living for a short time in England, where he published his first poems, he returned to live on a farm in New Hampshire. He won the Pulitzer Prize three times. Despite increasingly poor health, he wrote poetry to the end of his life. His last collection, *In the Clearing*, appeared in 1962, a year before his death.

Carole E. Gregory
She teaches writing at the Borough of Manhattan Community College and at New York University.

Adrian Henri
Born at Birkenhead, Cheshire in 1932, Adrian Henri attended grammar school in North Wales. He obtained a B.A. in Fine Art from Durham University in 1955. He moved to Liverpool in 1957 and became interested in poetry in 1961 when he first met Roger McGough and other Liverpool poets. From 1967 to 1970, he led the poetry/rock group 'Liverpool Scene'. Since 1970 he has been a freelance poet/painter/singer/songwriter. His paintings have been exhibited widely.

Langston Hughes
Black American novelist, short story writer, poet and playwright, Langston Hughes was born in Joplin, Missouri in 1902. He attended Columbia University in 1921 but left to participate in the more lively activity in nearby Harlem. He was celebrated early as a young poet of the Harlem Renaissance. During the 1930s he embraced radical politics. He died in 1967.

Elizabeth Jennings
Born in Boston, Lincolnshire, in 1926, Elizabeth Jennings was educated at Oxford High School and St. Anne's College, Oxford. After working as a librarian and a publisher's reader, she became a free-lance writer in 1961. Her collections of poetry include *Collected Poems*, Macmillan 1970 and *Celebrations and Elegies* 1982, Carcanet Press. Her second *Collected Poems*, 1986, won the W. H. Smith Literary Prize of 1987.

Meiling Jin
Born in Guyana, Meiling Jin now lives in London and is committed to fighting all forms of racism and sexism. She teaches women's self-defence and likes writing for children.

Denise Levertov
Born in Britain in 1923 of a Russian-Jewish father and a Welsh mother, Denise Levertov moved to the USA in 1948. In 1961 she became poetry editor of *The Nation*. Since then she has concentrated increasingly on political and feminist themes.

Roger McGough
Born in Liverpool in 1937, and educated at the University of Hull, Roger McGough taught for three years before entering the pop world and the Liverpool poets' scene. Since then he has written for stage and television.

Judith Nichols
Born in a farming community in Lincolnshire,
Judith Nichols went to school in a seaside
resort on the east coast. After spending some
time travelling, she settled in Wiltshire with
her husband and three children. She taught for
several years before becoming a full-time
writer. She is now in her mid-forties.

Theodore Roethke
Born in Michigan in 1908, Theodore Roethke's
first volume of poetry, *Open House*, was
published in 1941. He received the Pulitzer
Prize in 1954 and the Bollingen Prize in 1958.
He was awarded the National Book Award in
1959 for *Words for the Wind The collected
Verse of Theodore Roethke*. He died in 1963.

Ulrich Schaffer
Born in Germany but moved to Canada at the
age of ten. He now lives with his family in
British Columbia. He writes in English and
German.

Stevie Smith
Born in 1902 in Hull, she moved to Palmer's
Green, London, at the age of three and lived
there for the rest of her life. She worked all her
life for the magazine publishers Newnes-
Pearson, published her first novel in 1936, and
in all published eight collections of poetry. She
was well-known for her public readings and
recordings of her poetry. She died in 1971 and
her *Collected Poems* appeared posthumously in
1975.

Humbert Wolfe
Born in Italy in 1886. His family came to
England and settled in Bradford. He studied at
Wadham College, Oxford. In 1908 he entered
the civil service in the Board of Trade, later
moving to the Ministry of Labour where he had
a very successful career. He died in 1940. In his
literary work he believed strongly in the power
of poetry to convey good, and, through satire,
to rebuke evil.

Let's Talk About It

I know
that you think
you know
what is good for me,
but
I also think
that I know
what is good for me.

I know
you mean well,
but
I also mean well
for myself,
and in the end
I have to live my life.

Can we talk about it
and come up with something better
than either your or my opinion?

Ulrich Schaffer

Living

The fire in leaf and grass
so green it seems
each summer the last summer.

The wind blowing, the leaves
shivering in the sun,
each day the last day.

A red salamander
so cold and so
easy to catch, dreamily

moves his delicate feet
and long tail. I hold
my hand open for him to go.

Each minute the last minute

Denise Levertov

The Telephone Call

They asked me 'Are you sitting down?
Right? This is Universal Lotteries',
they said. 'You've won the top prize,
the Ultra-super Global Special.
What would you do with a million pounds?
Or, actually, with more than a million —
not that it makes a lot of difference
once you're a millionaire.' And they laughed.

'Are you OK?' they asked—'Still there?
Come on, now, tell us, how does it feel?'
I said 'I just . . . I can't believe it!'
They said 'That's what they all say.
What else? Go on, tell us about it.'
I said 'I feel the top of my head
has floated off, out through the window,
revolving like a flying saucer.'

'That's unusual' they said. 'Go on.'
I said 'I'm finding it hard to talk.
My throat's gone dry, my nose is tingling.
I think I'm going to sneeze—or cry.'
'That's right' they said, 'don't be ashamed
of giving way to your emotions.
It isn't every day you hear
you're going to get a million pounds.

Relax, now, have a little cry;
we'll give you a moment . . . ' 'Hang on!' I said.
'I haven't bought a lottery ticket
for years and years. And what did you say
the company's called?' They laughed again.
'Not to worry about a ticket.
We're Universal. We operate
a Retrospective Chances Module.

Nearly everyone's bought a ticket
in some lottery or another,
once at least. We buy up the files,
feed the names into our computer,
and see who the lucky person is.'
'Well, that's incredible' I said.
'It's marvellous. I still can't quite . . .
I'll believe it when I see the cheque.'

'Oh,' they said. 'there's no cheque.'
'But the money?' 'We don't deal in money.
Experiences are what we deal in.
You've had a great experience, right?
Exciting? Something you'll remember?
That's your prize. So congratulations
from all of us at Universal.
Have a nice day!' And the line went dead.

Fleur Adcock